MAKE POVERTY HISTORY

Nicky Gumbel

Alpha International
Holy Trinity Brompton
London

First published 2005
Reprint 2005 [once]

ISBN 1-904074-82-0

Published by Alpha International, Holy Trinity Brompton, Brompton Road, London, SW7 1JA

MAKE POVERTY HISTORY

On one occasion an expert in the law stood up to test Jesus. 'Teacher,' he asked, 'what must I do to inherit eternal life?'

'What is written in the Law?' he replied. 'How do you read it?'

He answered: '"Love the Lord your God with all your heart and with all your soul and with all your strength and with all your mind"; and, "Love your neighbour as yourself."'

'You have answered correctly,' Jesus replied. 'Do this and you will live.'

But he wanted to justify himself, so he asked Jesus, 'And who is my neighbour?'

In reply Jesus said: 'A man was going down from Jerusalem to Jericho, when he fell into the hands of robbers. They stripped him of his clothes, beat him and went away, leaving him half-dead. A priest happened to be going down the same road, and when he saw the man, he passed by on the other side. So too, a Levite, when he came to the place and saw him, passed by on the other side. But a Samaritan, as he travelled, came where the man was; and when he saw him, he took pity on him. He went to him and bandaged his wounds, pouring on oil and wine. Then he put the man on his own donkey, brought him to an inn and took care of him. The next day he took out two silver coins and gave them to the innkeeper. "Look after him," he said, "and when I return, I will reimburse you for any extra expense you may have."

'Which of these three do you think was a neighbour to the man who fell into the hands of robbers?'

The expert in the law replied, 'The one who had mercy on him.'

Jesus told him, 'Go and do likewise' (Luke 10:25–37).

2005 presents us all with an extraordinary opportunity to do something about arguably the greatest moral and ethical issue of our day: extreme poverty. Bono, the U2 rock star, started his speech at the Labour Party Conference in Brighton in September 2004 by saying:

My name is Bono and I'm a rock star. Brighton-rock-star.

Excuse me if I appear a little nervous. I'm not used to appearing before crowds of less than 80,000 people.

I heard the word party – obviously got the wrong idea.[1]

Bono went on to describe the month he spent working at an orphanage in Ethiopia:

On our last day at the orphanage a man handed me his baby and said, 'Take him with you'. He knew in Ireland his son would live; in Ethiopia his son would die. I turned him down.

In that moment, I started this journey.

In that moment, I became the worst thing of all:

a rock star with a cause.

Except this isn't a cause. 6,500 Africans dying a day of treatable, preventable disease, dying for want of medicines you and I can get at our local chemist. That's not a cause, that's an emergency.[1]

I am hesitant about approaching this subject, firstly because I run the risk of being a hypocrite. The second risk is best summarised by a quote from *The Simpsons*. When Homer Simpson asks his fundamentalist neighbours where they have been on holiday, they reply, 'We were at Bible camp – we were learning how to be more judgmental'.[2] That is certainly not my aim in this booklet.

Who are the poor?

The Bible describes two different types of poverty: material poverty and spiritual poverty. Each type can be divided into two: good and bad – so in all there are four different types of poverty.[3]

1. Bad spiritual poverty

In the parable of the Good Samaritan, Jesus says that the first command is to 'Love the Lord your God'. We have been created to live in a relationship with God and this will bring meaning, purpose, joy and peace to our lives. We experience 'bad spiritual poverty' if we lack this relationship with God and fail to recognise our need for him. Jesus says to the church in Revelation 3:17: 'You say, "I am rich; I have acquired wealth and do not need a thing." But you do not realise that you are wretched, pitiful, [spiritually] poor, blind and naked.' Jesus warns that if we have material riches it is hard to retain an attitude of dependence and humility: 'It is easier for a camel to go through the eye of a needle than for the rich to enter the kingdom of God' (Mark 10:25). Material things cannot satisfy. Jesus said, 'People do not live on bread alone, but on every word that comes from the mouth of God' (Matthew 4:4). When we drift away from our relationship with God, then whatever our material wealth, we experience bad spiritual poverty.

2. Good spiritual poverty

Jesus said, 'Blessed are the poor in spirit, for theirs is the kingdom of heaven' (Matthew 5:3). Good spiritual poverty comes from a recognition of our need for God. It is the opposite of an attitude of pride and self-sufficiency, which says, 'I can do without God'. Jesus tells us to 'Love the Lord your God with all your heart and with all your soul and with all your mind and with all your strength,' and 'Love your neighbour as yourself' (Mark 12:30–31). Good spiritual poverty says, 'Oh God, how can I do that? I make such a mess of my life. I certainly don't love you with all my heart and I don't love my neighbour as myself. Please be merciful to me.' Because of what Jesus has done for us on the cross it is possible for us to be forgiven and set free to live in relationship with God. Often those who are materially poor find it easier to recognise their need for God and to cry out to him for mercy. This desire to seek God, whoever we are and whatever our circumstances, is good spiritual poverty.

3. Good material poverty

Good material poverty is a kind of voluntary poverty, like that of Jesus. Paul says, 'For you know the grace of our Lord Jesus Christ, that though he was rich, yet for your sakes he became [materially] poor, so that you through his poverty might become [spiritually] rich' (2 Corinthians 8:9). When we have experienced the grace and love of God, our response is to say to the Lord, 'Here is my life. I want to give you everything I have.' And God calls some people, literally, to give away all their material possessions. This is a call and a gift, listed in 1 Corinthians 13 along with other gifts such as tongues and prophecy. This is a deeply challenging calling and a beautiful gift, but, as we see in the Bible, not everybody has that gift: Joseph of Arimathea was a rich man; Zacchaeus gave away half, but presumably he kept half, and Jesus asked the rich ruler to give away all that he had (Luke 18:18–23). All of us are called to be generous givers, and all of us are commanded not to judge. We are not to look at those wealthier than ourselves and say,

'They should be giving away all their money' – God may have called them to make money, to have money and to give generously. Rather, we are to ask for God's help and guidance as we decide how and what to give away ourselves.

4. Bad material poverty

When the Bible talks about 'the poor', it is generally referring to bad material poverty. This is a dehumanising poverty which must be combated. The man in the parable of the Good Samaritan is a kind of picture of the extreme poverty that exists in the world today. Robbed, stripped, beaten and half-dead, he is unable to help himself. Perhaps he is to blame: he should never have been walking down the road from Jerusalem to Jericho on his own with all those possessions. Perhaps, but this is not the point: the guy needs help. The people who would have been expected to go to his aid find themselves rather tied up with other things. People at the time would have been surprised that in Jesus' story it is the Samaritan who comes to help him, just as today people may be a little surprised that it is a rock star who is leading the campaign against poverty. Indeed, I think Bono himself is a little surprised to find it is a rock star who is leading this campaign.

What is the scale of this problem?

Poverty and inequality now exist on an unprecedented scale in world history. Bono talked about the difference between the south and the north, the 'have nots' and the 'have yachts'.[1] Of course, there are millions of people in the UK living in relative poverty and that is something that we must address. But I do not think anyone would argue that the extent and depth of poverty in the UK is similar to that in developing countries. For example, in the UK the average income is about £60 per day. More than half the world's population live on less than £1.20 a day, and 800 million people live on less than one dollar a day. They go to bed hungry every night. If you and I were to eat bread and water for the rest of our lives, we would be vastly better off than they are. Every three seconds poverty takes a child's life. Today and every day until we act, 30,000 children die because of avoidable diseases or because they live in poverty. Eight thousand people die of AIDS every day in developing countries. There will be 15 million preventable deaths this year.

Personal giving and the work of charitable organisations are essential, but poverty has now reached the stage where something else is required if our generation is to see any improvement in these statistics. Just by way of example, Tearfund is one of the biggest charitable organisations in the UK. In 2003–4 Tearfund raised around £35 million, which is amazing. But the interest on the debt of Sub-Saharan Africa is £27 million pounds a day. So within a week they have paid back five times more than Tearfund raised in an entire year.

Last year I visited an orphanage in Zambia where all the children have lost either one or both parents through AIDS. At the school the children are fed five times a week. Zambia is one of the richer countries and these are the lucky ones because every day they get a bowl of meal. Each bowl costs 16 pence. They have enough money to feed the children on Monday, Tuesday, Wednesday, Thursday and Friday. They get nothing on Saturday and Sunday. This is a relatively wealthy country, rich in natural resources. But every penny of profit from Zambia's copper mines, the main industry, is spent on repaying debt. Zambia spends twice as much on repaying its debt as it does on education. The country has average class sizes of 70 children and there are 8,000 unemployed teachers who the government simply cannot afford to employ.

Bono describes this fatal combination of debt and unfair trade, saying:

> Trade.
>
> Our badge of shame.

> We in the rich countries shuffle the poorest into a backroom, tie their hands and feet with our conditionalities and then use our subsidies to deliver the final blow.[1]

Just by way of example, EU citizens support the dairy industry to the tune of 16 billion euros a year – the equivalent of US$2.20 per cow per day. This means that the average EU cow now receives a subsidy amounting to more than the income of half the world's population.

The result is, of course, an extremely unfair playing field. This was demonstrated by a group of churches in Hertfordshire in June 2003. They put on a soccer match to demonstrate the impact of unfair trade rules. On the toss of the coin, the 'rich' team chose ends and took the kick-off. The rich countries only had a miniature goal to defend, while the poor countries struggled to defend a full-size goal. Their goalkeeper, representing Tanzania, had his hands tied behind his back, and their defenders, representing India and Uganda, were tied together as a three-legged pair. The referee, representing the World Trade Organisation, wore a patch over one eye and showed a distinct bias towards the rich nations, announcing extra rules for poor countries and insisting that they keep the ball below head height. A three-year-old, representing Bangladesh, took a penalty kick. By the end of the first half, in spite of the valiant efforts of the poor countries, the rich countries were in the lead by eight goals to nil, a score which the referee then doubled.[4]

Why do we need to act?

Some Christians through the ages have argued that because telling people about Jesus is so important, we should concentrate on that. So what is the theological and biblical basis for taking action against poverty? The Bible has much to say on the matter, but in essence there is a trinitarian basis for action. The first point is the nature and character of God. God is our Creator and every human being is of infinite value to him. Father Raniero Cantalamessa uses this analogy: Suppose we are watching a report of a disaster somewhere in the world and then we see on the television screen our son or daughter or brother, sister, mother or father. What a different attitude we would feel at that moment.[5] The point of the parable that Jesus told is that our neighbour refers not to an exclusive group of people, but to everyone. Bono says, 'You see, deep down, if we really accepted that Africans were equal to us, we would all do more to put the fire out'.[1]

God is a God of love but he is also a God of justice. All the way through the Old Testament, the Law and Prophets, the theme of justice recurs. There is an emphasis on legal justice, but also on social justice for the poor. Amos talks about the sins of Israel: 'They trample on the heads of the poor as upon the dust of the ground and deny justice to the oppressed... You trample on the poor and force them to give you grain...you deprive the poor of justice... I will not listen... But let justice roll on like a river, righteousness like a never-failing stream!' (Amos 2:7; 5:11, 12, 23, 24)

The second point is the example of Jesus. In Luke 9 when Jesus saw that the crowds were hungry, he fed them. In Luke 10 when the lawyer asked, 'Who is my neighbour?' Jesus taught the absolute and unlimited nature of the duty of love. At the time of Auschwitz many people said, 'We never knew, we weren't aware of what was going on'. No one can make that claim about starvation today because it is on our television screens. We can see it and we have a responsibility to act. When Jesus told the parable of the sheep and the goats, he said that one day he will say to the sheep:

> 'For I was hungry and you gave me something to eat, I was thirsty and you gave me something to drink, I was a stranger and you invited me in, I needed clothes and you clothed me, I was sick and you looked after me, I was in prison and you came to visit me.' Then the righteous will answer him, 'Lord, when did we see you hungry and feed you, or thirsty and give you something to drink? When did we see you a stranger and invite you in, or needing clothes and clothe you? When did we see you sick or in prison and

> go to visit you?' The King will reply, 'I tell you the truth, whatever you did for one of the least of these brothers and sisters of mine, you did for me' (Matthew 25:35–40).

Every time we minister to a poor person, we encounter Jesus. That is what makes it so exciting. The Chaplain General of the Prison Service, William Noblett, once said to me that he embarked on his career thinking that he was going to take Jesus into the prisons. But then he realised that Jesus was there already. Now, every time he goes into the prisons, he goes there to meet Jesus.

The third point is the work of the Holy Spirit. When the Spirit of God came upon Jesus he was filled with the Holy Spirit, and he read this from Isaiah: 'The Spirit of the Lord is on me, because he has anointed me to preach good news to the poor' (Luke 4:18). One of the first marks of the experience of the Spirit is a desire to make a difference to the poor.

What can we do?

Firstly, we can pray. Ignatius of Loyola said, 'Pray as if everything depended on God: work as if everything depended on you'.[6] I believe that 200 years ago slavery was an equivalent issue to that of poverty today and this movement was founded on prayer.

Secondly, we can take strategic action. I believe we need a change in social structures, which will in turn require a campaign for social justice, just as slavery did. It would have been a good thing for people to say, 'I'm going to let my slaves go'. That would have been a wonderful example, but the abolition of slavery took a campaign to bring it to an end. Similarly we need a wide vision as we consider how poverty can be alleviated. Although the rich countries have promised to halve poverty by the year 2015, they are not on course to fulfil their goal. The Chancellor, Gordon Brown, speaking in January 2005 said that the UN programme for poverty made certain promises. At best, on present progress in Sub-Saharan Africa the Millennium Development Goals (primary education for all, the halving of poverty and the elimination of avoidable infant deaths) will not all be fulfilled until 2165 – that is 150 years late. He went on to say, 'Africans know that it is often necessary to be patient, but the whole world should now know that 150 years is too long to ask people to wait for justice'.[7]

What excites me about the campaign to Make Poverty History is that it is not based purely on fundraising, but is a campaign for social justice. It is best summed up in these three phrases – **'trade justice', 'drop the debt' and 'more and better aid'.**

Trade justice – This is not a kind of naïve idealism. *The Sunday Times* leader on 9 January 2005 said this:

> The [Make Poverty History] campaign's call for trade justice is hard to fault. Africa is the continent that trade liberalisation left behind. In 25 years its share of world trade has dropped from 5% to less than 2%. Africa is hugely dependent on agriculture and has been particularly vulnerable to the protectionist farm policies. The appalling Common Agricultural Policy which combines discrimination against poor countries' exports and dumping of agricultural products in their markets has wrought havoc. African farmers have seen their livelihoods destroyed. The United Nations estimate these and other unfair trade practices cost poor countries US$400 billion a year. Make Poverty History is right to urge governments to make global trade fair for the world's poor. [8]

Drop the debt – This means cancelling the poorest countries' unpayable debts. The very small amount of debt that has already been cancelled has had a huge impact on these countries. For example, in Uganda, four million more children have been able to go to primary school. In Tanzania, 31,000 new classrooms have been built and 18,000 new teachers recruited. In Mozambique, half a million children are now being vaccinated against tetanus, whooping cough and diphtheria. But there is much more to do. The vision of Make Poverty History is to double aid and halve poverty. The Chancellor Gordon Brown said, 'To insist on the payment of these debts is unjust – it offends human dignity. What is morally wrong cannot be economically right'.[9]

More and better aid – Gordon Brown said this:

> As many as half of all malaria deaths could be prevented if people had access to diagnosis and drugs that cost no more than 12 cents. A quarter of all child deaths could be prevented if children slept beneath bed-nets costing $4 each. $3 more for each new mother could save up to 5 million lives over the next ten years.[9]

The generous public response to the Tsunami disaster has been amazing, but this wave of generosity must now be directed to places where the need is just as great, but perhaps less visible.

What about corruption? I love what Bono says about that argument: 'All of you have to double aid, double its effectiveness, and double trouble for corrupt leaders'.[1]

2005 is a year of unique opportunity. Among other things, it is the twentieth anniversary of Live Aid, the EU presidency is with the UK for the second half of the year, and there is the G8 summit, hosted by the UK in Scotland this July. Poverty will be a main topic of discussion at G8 and, humanly speaking, this is the place for action. Eight men in one room have the power to change the world. But this cannot happen without mass movement at the grass roots level. Nelson Mandela said, 'It is not the Kings and Generals who make history but the masses of the people'.[10] That's what Bono and others are trying to stimulate in this country and around the world this year. Bono again:

> Now you know why Tony Blair and Gordon Brown are really excited that U2's got a new album coming out – why?
>
> Because I'll be away on tour next year.
>
> But even from a tour bus I can be a pain in the neck (arse). That's my job. And I've got some very interesting friends, there's as many of them in mothers' unions as trade unions.
>
> It's not just purple Mohawks we've got going, it's blue rinses.
>
> It's the Temperance League of Tunbridge Wells.
>
> The Wigan Bowling Society.
>
> The Chipping Camden Ladies' Cricket Club.
>
> OK, I made those up. But don't mess with us.[1]

As Father Raniero Cantalamessa put it, 'What we need today is...a mass mobilisation of all – indeed of the whole civilised world – to liberate those living tombs of Christ who are the millions upon millions of people dying of hunger, disease and want'.[11]

I started with the words of Bono at the Labour Party Conference and I want to finish with the end of his speech:

> If Britain can't turn its values into action against extreme, stupid poverty... if this rich country, with the reins in its hands, can't lead other countries along this path to equality, then the critics tomorrow will be right...
>
> Listen, this is a real moment coming up, this could be real history, this could be something that your children, your children's children, that our whole generation, will be remembered for at the beginning of the 21st century...
>
> This is not about 'doing our best'.
>
> It's win or lose.
>
> Life or death.
>
> Literally so. If I could ask you to think a hundred years ahead, to imagine what we, and our times, will be remembered for, I would venture three things:
>
> the Internet,
>
> the war on terror,
>
> and the fate of the continent of Africa.
>
> We are the first generation that can look extreme and stupid poverty in the eye, look across the water to Africa and elsewhere and say this and mean it:
>
> we have the cash,
>
> we have the drugs,

we have the science – but do we have the will?
Do we have the will to make poverty history?
Some say we can't afford to.
I say we can't afford not to.[1]

For more information please see:

makepovertyhistory.org

Notes

1. Bono, from his speech at the Labour Party Conference in Brighton, 29 September 2004.
2. *The Simpsons*, from the episode *Bart of Darkness*, FOX Broadcasting Company, September 1994.
3. Raniero Cantalamessa, *Poverty* (Alba House, 1997), p.xi.
4. *Christian Aid, Trade Justice – A Christian Response to Global Poverty* (Church House Publishing, 2004).
5. Raniero Cantalamessa, *Poverty* (Alba House, 1997), p.4.
6. Attributed to St Ignatius Loyola, cf. Joseph de Guibert, SJ, *The Jesuits: Their Spiritual Doctrine and Practice* (Chicago: Loyola University Press, 1964), p.148, n.55.
7. The Rt Hon Gordon Brown MP, Chancellor of the Exchequer, from his speech at the Commission for Africa meeting, Cape Town, 17 January 2005.
8. *The Sunday Times*, 9 January 2005.
9. Speech by Gordon Brown MP, Chancellor of the Exchequer, at the National Gallery of Scotland, 6 January 2005.
10. Nelson Mandela, from his speech at the Soweto Homecoming Rally, 11 February 1990.
11. Raniero Cantalamessa, *Poverty* (Alba House, 1997), p.19.